AF870559

Dave Ramsey's

Financial Peace UNIVERSITY

INFORMATION GUIDE

MISSION STATEMENT:

To empower and give HOPE to everyone from the financially secure to the financially distressed.

What Others Are Saying About FPU

"Let me say it straight up--Financial Peace University has, quite literally, changed the way our congregation handles money. With hundreds of our people in the training, we have experienced a noticeable difference in... well, frankly, in finances and in peace. That's because FPU is both biblical and practical. Further, because it strengthens marriages and families, a universal need, FPU has actually become an outreach mechanism for us. It's a win, win, win."

Stu Webber
Author and Pastor
Good Shepherd Community Church

"As a pastor, I saw many needs in our church, from families in disarray due to financial issues to young people graduating from college in debt without a plan. Financial Peace University helped 200 families in our congregation pay off over $733,000 and save over $192,000!"

Bishop Joseph W. Walker, III
Pastor, Mt. Zion Baptist Church

"I wish we could give it as a wedding gift to every couple that we know as they're crossing that proverbial threshold. Make sure you go through Financial Peace University. Become a graduate, walk away with your diploma of terrific skills that will last you a lifetime and benefit your marriage."

Drs. Les and Leslie Parrott
Best-selling Authors and Marriage Experts

"One of the things that I love about Financial Peace University are the baby steps. They don't have to do it all at once. They just gotta take one baby step at a time, and I love sharing with them that if you'll just enroll in this course, and just take baby step one, you'll experience some freedom and some relief and you'll be encouraged to take baby step two..."

Bob Shelton
Director of Stewardship
Baptist General Convention of Oklahoma

About the Founder of FPU

Dave Ramsey, a personal money management expert, is an extremely popular national radio personality, author of the New York Times best-sellers *The Total Money Makeover, Financial Peace* and *More Than Enough*, and the founder of Financial Peace University. Ramsey knows first-hand what financial peace means in his own life – living a true rags-to-riches, back-to-rags, back-to-riches story. By age twenty-six he had established a four-million-dollar real estate portfolio, only to lose it by age thirty. He has since rebuilt his financial life and now devotes himself full-time to helping ordinary people understand the forces behind their financial distress and how to set things right – financially, emotionally and spiritually. He resides with his wife Sharon and their three children in Nashville, Tennessee.

TABLE OF CONTENTS

What Is FPU?

Financial Peace University is a tool that supports churches by equipping them with a biblically-based accountability class that will teach and train their congregation and community to manage their resources. The class is taught by Dave Ramsey, via DVD, followed by a small group discussion. We suggest each session last 2 hours: video 1 hour; small group 1 hour.

TEACHING: Did you know that there are over 800 Scriptures regarding personal finance? FPU teaches stewardship - how to manage 100% of what God has given. Dave Ramsey does all the teaching on 13 video lessons.

Lesson 1 - **Super Savers -** Proverbs 6:6-9
Common Sense for Your Dollars and Cents

Lesson 2 - **Relating with Money -** Matthew 6:21
Nerds and Free Spirits Unite!

Lesson 3 - **Cash Flow Planning -** Luke 14:28-30
The Nuts and Bolts of Budgeting

Lesson 4 - **Dumping Debt -** Proverbs 22:7
Breaking the Chains of Debt

Lesson 5 - **Swimming with Sharks -** Proverbs 3:27
Understanding Credit Bureaus and Collection Practices

Lesson 6 - **Buyer Beware -** Proverbs 10:22
The Power of Marketing on Your Buying Decisions

Lesson 7 - **Clause and Effect -** Proverbs 27:12
The Role of Insurance in Your Financial Plan

Lesson 8 - **That's Not Good Enough! -** Proverbs 11:1
How to Buy Only Big, Big Bargains

Lesson 9 - **Of Mice and Mutual Funds -** Proverbs 21:5
Understanding Investments

Lesson 10 - **From Fruition to Tuition -** Proverbs 13:22
Planning for Retirement and College

Lesson 11 - **Working in Your Strengths -** 1 Peter 4:10
Careers and Extra Jobs

Lesson 12 - **Real Estate and Mortgages -** Proverbs 24:27
Keeping the American Dream from Becoming a Nightmare

Lesson 13 - **The Great Misunderstanding -** Psalm 24:1
Unleashing the Power of Generous Giving

Small Groups: Following the video, a volunteer hosts a small group discussion. In the small group, behavior change occurs most effectively. The group members encourage one another to apply the principles they are learning. Together, the group discovers the seven Baby Steps needed to walk in financial peace. The objective of the small group is not to know everyone's business; it is helping each other apply the principles.

> Personal finance is 80% behavior and 20% knowledge.

The Benefits of FPU

How will my church benefit from FPU?

- **The average family pays off $5,300 and saves $2,700 during the 13 week period.**
- **Financial stress is reduced.**
- **Couples begin to communicate.**
- **Singles are empowered.**
- **Dave's common-sense approach to personal finance makes FPU a tremendous outreach tool.**
- **Families begin to "do" the Biblical principles because application is emphasized throughout the class.**
- **FPU strengthens your congregation by teaching them how to handle their finances, enabling them to give like never before.**
- **Biblical stewardship is woven through all 13 lessons, guiding families to manage 100% of their resources.**
- **Families discover the power of generous giving.**

Imagine what the people of God could do for the Kingdom of God if they were debt free.

- ❑ **Visit the Coordinator Resource Center (CRC) online for tons of information on planning and promoting your class.**
  - Visit the CRC at daveramsey.com/fpucoordinator

- ❑ **Familiarize yourself with this book and the Info CD/DVD.**
  - Call your advisor at 877-378-2667 with any questions.
  - Select 2 dates for an FPU Free Preview & Class Start Date.

- ❑ **Meet with a decision maker to get approval to start FPU.**
  - Share your vision for Financial Peace University.
  - Show the FPU Introduction video (4 min).
  - Recommend the selected start dates.
  - Read and sign Licensing Agreement online in the CRC or fax it to your advisor.
  - Go online to the CRC and enter your "Free Preview" dates and start date or call your advisor at 877-378-2667.

- ❑ **Promote! Promote! Promote!**
  - Visit the CRC online for great resources to promote your class!
  - For helpful tips, see "How To Promote Your Class" on the CD-ROM.

- ❑ **Hold 'Free Preview(s)' and enroll families.**
  - See Preview Outline on page 14.

- ❑ **Order your materials by doing one of the following.**
  - Go online to daveramsey.com/fpucoordinator
  - Call your advisor at 877-378-2667.

- ❑ **Start your class!**
  - Allow 7-10 business days for materials to arrive.

Your FPU Class Materials

Membership Kit - $93

Financial Peace University Workbook
13 life-changing lessons that walk you step by step through the FPU program.

Audio CD Library
Includes all 13 lessons, PLUS two bonus CDs - Dave's Personal Testimony and the Best of *The Dave Ramsy Show*!

Budgeting Forms
A complete set of reproducible monthly budgeting forms with full instructions and examples.

Two FPU Bonus CD-ROMs
Financial Calculators, screensavers, financial management forms, and more! PLUS, an extra disc to share with a friend!

Debit Card Holders
Protects you and your card by reminding you that your financial peace depends on your behavior.

Dave's Best-Selling Book
Over a million people have benefited from these solid financial principles of common-sense money management!

FPU Envelope System
Dave's famous, easy-to-use cash management envelope system - a great tool to organize your money and stay on budget.

Tip Cards
A handy tip calculator with Dave's Seven Baby Steps on the other side! Plus, we've included extras to give away!

Leadership Kit - $299

Leadership Kit includes
Everything in the Membership Kit, plus the items listed below:

DVD Video Series
Dave's complete video library PLUS a promotional orientation DVD—everything you need to begin sharing FPU with your community!

FPU Facilitator Guide
A step-by-step guide to assist you in leading the FPU small group sessions.

Promotional Brochures
One set (50 count) of informative brochures that explain the benefits of FPU—a great resource to help publicize your upcoming class!

Much More!
When you register as an FPU Facilitator, your benefits go beyond what's included in this box! Go to daveramsey.com to learn more!

FPU Church Leadership Program Licensing Agreement

This is an arrangement between the accepting Church and The Lampo Group, Inc. (TLGI) for the public presentation and use of the video series titled Financial Peace University (FPU). The Financial Peace University series includes video lessons (Preview Video and 13 video lessons), all course materials, and Coordinator's Guide. The Church agrees to exhibit for enrolled FPU MEMBERS ONLY the Financial Peace University video series.

Since this class is strictly a discipleship program to assist people in managing and being good stewards of what God has given them, we have a few requirements for all FPU Coordinators or small group leaders.

1. If the Coordinator is employed or actively engaged for profit, directly or indirectly through family relationship or professional association, in any financial services industry, including but not limited to financial planning, insurance, or securities, they can not in any way approach class members with their services or products.

2. If the Coordinator is directly or indirectly associated with any "multi-level" or "network" marketing organizations, they can not recruit or sell to Financial Peace University members.

3. The Coordinator may be privy to confidential financial and personal details of FPU members in their class. The Coordinator pledges 100% confidentiality on such matters.

4. The Coordinator will not divulge any FPU member information to outside parties other than TLGI phone advisors or counselors, without the particular "FPU" member's consent by written authorization.

5. The Coordinator will follow the FPU program process as described in the Financial Peace University Coordinator's Guide. Coordinator may not change or modify the way the FPU program is presented or conducted without the prior express written consent of TLGI.

6. The Coordinator may not edit, transfer to another format, add to, or alter in any way the Financial Peace University videos or any of the FPU materials.

7. The Coordinator may not enter into any arrangements or make any representation or pledge which may infer liability or cause financial responsibility on behalf of TLGI or FPU, it's suppliers, employees, or assigns.

FPU Licensing Agreement (Continued)

Ordering FPU Membership Materials: The Church agrees to purchase 1 (one) Membership kit per family unit enrolling in FPU (allow 7-10 days for delivery). (Family unit consists of spouse and teenage children who are living with their parents.)

1. A family unit is defined as a single adult individual, a married couple, or an engaged couple who has set a date for getting married within one year of their enrollment.
2. A married couple is defined as a male and female joined in accordance with the state laws of Tennessee.

General Information: This Church Arrangement shall be construed, interpreted, and governed by the laws of the State of Tennessee. This arrangement and any waiver(s) attached constitute the full and complete arrangement binding the parties, and will be enforced to the full extent permitted under applicable law. TLGI retains all rights not specifically granted herein. If any provision is declared invalid or unenforceable, all remaining provisions will nevertheless remain in effect. If you have any questions regarding this agreement, please consult your FPU advisor.

Church Name and City: ______________________________

Church Staff Signature: ______________________________

(Please Print Name) ____________________ Date Signed: ______________

Church Coordinator Signature: ______________________________

(Please Print Name) ____________________ Date Signed: ______________

Please send in a copy of this signed and dated form to The Lampo Group and provide the church with a signed copy.

Information and Promotion CD/DVD

Most of your promotional tools and resources are on the CD/DVD included with this booklet and in the Coordinator Resource Center online. Included in these tools are banners, posters, flyers, door-hangers, postcards, table tents, bulletin inserts and more. These can be printed at your local print shop. Some items, such as the 8.5 X 11 flyers and the postcards can be printed in-house.

Promotional Videos

You also have promotional videos available that you can use during announcement times at weekly services following up to the 'Free Preview'.

Brochures

You may also request a set of 50 preprinted color brochures and three preprinted color posters.

Testimonies

Allow those who have exprerienced the value of FPU for themselves to share their story.

Additional promotion ideas:

Newspaper Ads - You can trade out free advertising for one (1) FPU Membership Kit.

Local Radio Stations may help promote FPU, especially stations broadcasting The Dave Ramsey Show. Go to the Coordinator Resource Center at daveramsey.com/fpucoordinator and download our free radio spots.

Local TV Stations and Cable TV are always looking for stories they can follow or cover that are changing their community. You can invite them to attend the program and follow a family's progress throughout the program.

Public Service Announcements are usually FREE on church bulletin boards, computer bulletin boards, cable community access channels, community section of the newspaper, and local radio station community bulletin spots.

For a successful FPU promotional campaign, follow the Suggested Promotional Schedule on the next page.

Suggested Promotional Schedule

SIX WEEKS TO PREVIEW MEETING:

Print promotional items from the Promo CD/DVD at your local print shop or in-house.

FOUR WEEKS TO PREVIEW:

Place posters, banners, doorhangers, table tents, etc. in strategic, high-traffic areas around your church and community. Send postcards to church attendees. Place an ad in the local newspaper; advertise on your church web site and newsletter.

THREE WEEKS TO PREVIEW:

Begin placing inserts in bulletins for church services. Also, show a one-minute video from the Promo CD/DVD. You may want to have a "high-influence" church leader announce the upcoming 'Free Preview'.

TWO WEEKS TO PREVIEW:

Continue with bulletin inserts. Show another promo video to your church. Have an email sent from the church to the congregation about the class.

ONE WEEK TO PREVIEW:

Have an FPU class graduate share a personal testimony, or show another promo video to your church assembly. Have another "high-influence" church leader announce the upcoming 'Free Preview'.

WEEK OF THE PREVIEW:

This is the optimal time for your minister to encourage the church to come to the Preview Meeting. For maximum impact, the minister might consider teaching on becoming debt-free for the Kingdom! FPU will then be a natural follow-up to your minister's vision.

AS YOUR CLASS BEGINS:

Encourage your class members to invite friends and family to an open-house during Lesson #5. Doing so will cultivate future ministry and get folks excited about joining your church's next class!

Fill in YOUR Promotional Schedule on the next page!

SIX WEEKS TO PREVIEW MEETING ______________________________

FIVE WEEKS TO PREVIEW MEETING ______________________________

FOUR WEEKS TO PREVIEW MEETING ______________________________

THREE WEEKS TO PREVIEW MEETING ______________________________

TWO WEEKS TO PREVIEW MEETING ______________________________

WEEK OF PREVIEW MEETING ______________________________

CLASS START ______________________________

The Free Preview

Prior to the Free Preview, please download and print a Class Enrollment Registration sheet from the Coordinator Resource Center at daveramsey.com/fpucoordinator

Introduction Information: (5 minutes)

- Welcome everyone and introduce yourself as the Class Coordinator.
- Be sure they understand that you are the host and facilitator of the program, NOT a financial instructor, advisor, or counselor.
- Dave Ramsey will be the instructor via video DVD.
- Tell them why you have become a volunteer FPU Coordinator.

Start the Preview Video Presentation (20 minutes)

- Play the FPU Church Preview all the way through.
- Ask the following discussion questions:

Why were the families in the video willing to make changes in their lives?

Hopefully you'll hear ..."They were serious about taking the steps necessary to getting out of debt, and staying out of debt, and building wealth God's way!"

How would it feel to manage your family's money and know you are making the right decisions?

Hopefully you'll hear ..."That would feel great!"

Are you willing to invest what you might spend on pizza and colas for a month in order to change your family tree?

You probably won't hear anything now ... that one was rhetorical.

Invite everyone to enroll in this Life Changing Program (10 minutes)

- The retail amount for the Member Kits is $299
- Church group discount is $93 (Shipping and handling is 7%. This amount can be added to the individual price or be paid by the church.)
- Let them know that you will be ordering the class materials based upon the number of enrollments.

Announce the time and day your 1st class will start (5 minutes)

- See if anyone has questions.
- See Preview Frequently Asked Questions Reference Sheet (right).

How often do the classes meet?

There are 13 class sessions meeting one day per week.

How long is each class session?

We suggest **two hours** for each session, and each is independent of the others.

Part One is taught by Dave Ramsey via video to help you learn how to make wise financial decisions based on Scripture.
Part Two of each class session is a SMALL CIRCLE group discussion.

The design of the small discussion groups helps you apply the principles to your daily life. The small group members will help hold each other accountable, and support one another. The discussion group will help insure we are working on the behavior part.

What is the average size of the class?

The video portion of the class is UNLIMITED. However, we recommend you break down into small groups of 8-12 families for the small group time with a coordinator/small group facilitator for each group.

What happens if I miss one class? Can I make it up?

The coordinator can work with you to make up that lesson by allowing you to take the video lesson home with you, as long as you will return it the following class. There may be a deposit required to borrow a lesson on DVD, depending on the coordinator.

What is included in the FPU Membership Kit? See Page 8

Can I get CEU's (Continuing Education Unit) for the class?

Yes, in many cases, FPU is accepted as CEU's.
Go to daveramsey.com for details.

Preview Frequently Asked Questions

What if people have a previous version of the FPU materials?

People with previous versions of FPU are considered Lifetime Members and may attend your class at no additional charge. If they would like to upgrade their materials, call your advisor for details.

When will the first class start?

Please give them your start date.
The FIRST CLASS SESSION usually takes place approximately TWO WEEKS after the final preview session, allowing time to process the enrollments and ship ALL the class materials.

Can your class member get additional assistance if they need it?

For more detailed, complex assistance, Dave Ramsey Certified Counselors offer discounts for one-on-one counseling. To find a counselor in your area go to daveramsey.com/fpu/counseling.

Who benefits from this program?

Everyone TRULY benefits from this program –
Regardless of your age. Regardless of your income.
Regardless of being single, married, divorced or a single parent.

How much does this program cost?

Materials retail for $299, church families pay $93 plus shipping and handling.

Who can attend with my Financial Peace membership?

Your spouse and teens living in the home.

Is there any refund if I do not like the program?

Our guarantee is simply this –

If you do it, **it works!** If you don't do it, **it won't work!**
If you work the program, **you won't want your money back!**
If you don't work the program, **you don't get your money back!**

Dave Ramsey's

Financial Peace UNIVERSITY

INFORMATION GUIDE

MISSION STATEMENT:

To empower and give HOPE to everyone from the financially secure to the financially distressed.

What Others Are Saying About FPU

"*Financial Peace University* has, quite literally, changed the way our congregation handles money. With hundreds of our people in the training, we have experienced a noticeable difference in finances and peace. That's because FPU is both biblical and practical. Further, because it strengthens marriages and families, FPU has actually become an outreach mechanism for us."

Stu Webber
Author and Pastor
Good Shepherd Community Church

"As a pastor, I saw many needs in our church, from families in disarray due to financial issues to young people graduating from college in debt without a plan. *Financial Peace University* helped 200 families in our congregation pay off over $733,000 and save over $192,000!"

Bishop Joseph W. Walker, III
Pastor, Mt. Zion Baptist Church

"I wish we could give it as a wedding gift to every couple that we know as they're crossing that proverbial threshold. Make sure you go through *Financial Peace University*. Become a graduate, walk away with your diploma of terrific skills that will last you a lifetime and benefit your marriage."

Drs. Les and Leslie Parrott
Best-selling Authors and Marriage Experts

"One of the things that I love about *Financial Peace University* is the Baby Step system. People don't have to do it all at once, they just have to take one step at a time. If you just enroll in this course and only reach Baby Step One, you'll experience some freedom and relief and then be encouraged to move on to Baby Step Two."

Bob Shelton
Director of Stewardship
Baptist General Convention of Oklahoma

About the Founder of FPU

Dave Ramsey, a personal money management expert, is an extremely popular national radio personality, author of the *New York Times* best-sellers *The Total Money Makeover, Financial Peace* and *More Than Enough*, and the founder of *Financial Peace University*. Ramsey knows first-hand what financial peace means in his own life—living a true rags-to-riches, back-to-rags, back-to-riches story. By age twenty-six he had established a four-million-dollar real estate portfolio, only to lose it by age thirty. He has since rebuilt his financial life and now devotes himself full-time to helping ordinary people understand the forces behind their financial distress and how to set things right—financially, emotionally and spiritually. He resides with his wife Sharon and their three children in Nashville, Tennessee.

TABLE OF CONTENTS

What Is FPU?

***Financial Peace University* is a tool that supports churches** by equipping them with a biblically-based accountability class that will train their congregation and community to manage their resources. The class is taught by Dave Ramsey via DVD, followed by a small group discussion. We suggest each session last two hours: one hour for the video lesson and one hour for the small group discussion.

TEACHING: Did you know that there are over 800 Scriptures regarding personal finance? FPU teaches stewardship—how to manage 100% of what God has given. Dave Ramsey does all the teaching on these 13 entertaining video lessons:

Lesson 1 – **Super Saving**
Common Sense for Your Dollars and Cents; Proverbs 6:6-9

Lesson 2 – **Relating With Money**
Nerds and Free Spirits Unite!; Matthew 6:21

Lesson 3 – **Cash Flow Planning**
The Nuts and Bolts of Budgeting; Luke 14:28-30

Lesson 4 – **Dumping Debt**
Breaking the Chains of Debt; Proverbs 22:7

Lesson 5 – **Credit Sharks In Suits**
Understanding Credit Bureaus and Collection Practices; Proverbs 3:27

Lesson 6 – **Buyer Beware**
The Power of Marketing on Your Buying Decisions; Proverbs 10:22

Lesson 7 – **Clause and Effect**
The Role of Insurance in Your Financial Plan; Proverbs 27:12

Lesson 8 – **That's Not Good Enough!**
How to Buy Only Big, Big Bargains; Proverbs 11:1

Lesson 9 – **Of Mice and Mutual Funds**
Understanding Investments; Proverbs 21:5

Lesson 10 – **From Fruition to Tuition**
Planning for Retirement and College; Proverbs 13:22

Lesson 11 – **Working In Your Strengths**
Careers and Extra Jobs; 1 Peter 4:10

Lesson 12 – **Real Estate and Mortgages**
Keeping the American Dream from Becoming a Nightmare; Proverbs 24:27

Lesson 13 – **The Great Misunderstanding**
Unleashing the Power of Generous Giving; Psalm 24:1

Small Groups: Following the video, a volunteer hosts a small group discussion. It is in the small group discussion where genuine behavior change takes place. The group members encourage one another to *apply* the principles they are learning. Together, the group works through the seven Baby Steps needed to walk in financial peace. The objective of the small group is not to pry into everyone's business; it is simply to walk together as each family learns and applies the principles.

Personal finance is **80% behavior** and only **20% head knowledge.**

How will my church benefit from FPU?

- The average family pays off $5,300 and saves $2,700 during the 13–week period.
- Financial stress is reduced.
- Couples begin to communicate about money, priorities, goals, and more.
- Singles are empowered and encouraged to find accountability partners.
- Dave's common-sense approach to personal finance makes FPU a tremendous outreach tool.
- Families begin to live out the biblical principles because application is emphasized throughout the class.
- FPU strengthens your congregation by teaching members how to handle their finances, enabling them to give like never before.
- Biblical stewardship is woven through all 13 lessons, guiding families to manage 100% of their resources.
- Families discover the power of generous giving.

Imagine what the **people of God** could do for the **Kingdom of God** if they were debt free.

- ❑ **Visit the Coordinator Resource Center (CRC) online for tons of information on planning and promoting your class.**
  - Visit the CRC at daveramsey.com/fpucoordinator.

- ❑ **Familiarize yourself with this book and the Promotion CD-ROM/DVD.**
  - Call your advisor at 877.378.2667 with any questions.
  - Schedule two FPU Free Preview dates and your Class Start Date.

- ❑ **Meet with a decision maker to get approval to start FPU.**
  - Share your vision for *Financial Peace University*.
  - Show the FPU Introduction video (4 minutes).
  - Recommend the selected start dates.
  - Read and accept the Licensing Agreement online in the CRC or fax it to your advisor.
  - Go online to the CRC and enter your FPU Free Preview dates and start date or call your advisor at 877.378.2667.

- ❑ **Promote! Promote! Promote!**
  - Visit the CRC online for great resources to promote your class!
  - For helpful tips, see "How To Promote Your Class" on the CD-ROM.

- ❑ **Hold the FPU Free Preview(s) and enroll families.**
  - See Preview Outline on page 14.

- ❑ **Order your materials by doing one of the following:**
  - Go online to daveramsey.com/fpucoordinator.
  - Call your advisor at 877.378.2667.

- ❑ **Start your class!**
  - Allow 7-10 business days for materials to arrive.

Your FPU Class Materials

Membership Kit - $93

Financial Peace University Workbook
13 life-changing lessons that walk you step by step through the FPU program.

Audio CD Library
Includes all 13 lessons, PLUS two bonus CDs–Dave's Personal Testimony and the Best of *The Dave Ramsey Show*!

Budgeting Forms
A complete set of reproducible monthly budgeting forms with full instructions and examples.

Two FPU Bonus CD-ROMs
Financial calculators, screensavers, financial management forms, and more! PLUS, an extra disc to share with a friend!

Dave's Best-Selling Book
Over a million people have benefited from these solid financial principles of common-sense money management!

FPU Envelope System
Dave's famous, easy-to-use cash management envelope system–a great tool to organize your money and stay on budget.

Tip Cards
A handy tip calculator with Dave's Seven Baby Steps on the other side! Plus, we've included extras to give away!

Debit Card Holders
Protects you and your card by reminding you that your financial peace depends on your behavior.

Leadership Kit - $299

Leadership Kit
Includes everything in the Membership Kit, plus the items listed below:

DVD Video Series
Dave's complete video library PLUS a promotional orientation DVD—everything you need to begin sharing FPU with your community!

FPU Coordinator Guide
A step-by-step guide to assist you in leading the FPU small group sessions.

Promotional Brochures
One set (50 count) of informative brochures that explain the benefits of FPU—a great resource to help publicize your upcoming class!

Much More!
When you register as an FPU Coordinator, your benefits go beyond what's included in this box! Go to daveramsey.com to learn more!

FPU Church Leadership Program Licensing Agreement

This is an arrangement between the accepting Church and The Lampo Group, Inc. (TLGI) for the public presentation and use of the video series titled *Financial Peace University* (FPU). The *Financial Peace University* series includes video lessons (Preview Video and 13 video lessons), all course materials, and Coordinator's Guide. The Church agrees to exhibit for enrolled FPU MEMBERS ONLY the *Financial Peace University* video series.

Since this class is strictly a discipleship program to assist people in managing and being good stewards of what God has given them, we have a few requirements for all FPU Coordinators or small group leaders.

1. If the Coordinator is employed or actively engaged for profit, directly or indirectly through family relationship or professional association, in any financial services industry, including but not limited to financial planning, insurance, or securities, they cannot in any way approach class members with their services or products.

2. If the Coordinator is directly or indirectly associated with any "multi-level" or "network" marketing organizations, they cannot recruit or sell to *Financial Peace University* members.

3. The Coordinator may be privy to confidential financial and personal details of FPU members in their class. The Coordinator pledges 100% confidentiality on such matters.

4. The Coordinator will not divulge any FPU member information to outside parties other than TLGI phone advisors or counselors without the particular FPU member's consent by written authorization.

5. The Coordinator will follow the FPU program process as described in the *Financial Peace University* Coordinator's Guide. The Coordinator may not change or modify the way the FPU program is presented or conducted without the prior express written consent of TLGI.

6. The Coordinator may not edit, transfer to another format, add to, or alter in any way the *Financial Peace University* videos or any of the FPU materials.

7. The Coordinator may not enter into any arrangements or make any representation or pledge which may infer liability or cause financial responsibility on behalf of TLGI or FPU, its suppliers, employees, or assigns.

FPU Licensing Agreement (Continued)

Copyright Notice: *Financial Peace University*, also referred to as FPU, is protected in whole and in part by U.S. copyright laws and international treaty provisions. All title and copyrights in and to *Financial Peace University*, including but not limited to any images, photographs, animations, video, audio, music, text, electronic applications and accompanying printed materials incorporated into *Financial Peace University* and any copies of *Financial Peace University* are owned by The Lampo Group, Inc.. No one is authorized to copy any *Financial Peace University* audio, video, lesson or Coordinator materials without the prior consent of the FPU Director, on behalf of The Lampo Group, Inc.. If violated, the Lampo Group, Inc. may at its discretion commence civil action seeking fines, attorneys' fees, injunctive relief, and, in appropriate circumstances, criminal prosecution with all reasonable legal and attorneys' fees to be paid by the Church.

Ordering FPU Membership Materials: The Church agrees to purchase one Membership kit per family unit enrolling in FPU (allow 7-10 days for delivery).

1. A family unit is defined as an individual, a married couple, or an engaged couple who has set a date for getting married within one year of their enrollment.
2. A married couple is defined as a male and female joined in accordance with the state laws of Tennessee.

General Information: This Church Licensing Agreement shall be construed, interpreted, and governed by the laws of the State of Tennessee. This arrangement and any waiver(s) attached constitute the full and complete arrangement binding the parties and will be enforced to the full extent permitted under applicable law. TLGI retains all rights not specifically granted herein. If any provision is declared invalid or unenforceable, all remaining provisions will nevertheless remain in effect. If you have any questions regarding this agreement, please consult your FPU advisor.

Church Name and City: ______________________________

Church Staff Signature: ______________________________

(Please Print Name) ____________________ Date Signed: ______________

Church Coordinator Signature: ______________________________

(Please Print Name) ____________________ Date Signed: ______________

Please send a copy of this signed and dated form to The Lampo Group and provide the church with a signed copy.

Information and Promotion CD/DVD

Most of your promotional tools and resources are on the CD/DVD included with this booklet and in the Coordinator Resource Center online. Included in these tools are banners, posters, flyers, doorhangers, postcards, table tents, bulletin inserts, and more. These can be printed at your local print shop. Some items, such as the 8.5 x 11 flyers and the postcards, can be printed in-house.

Promotional Videos

You also have promotional videos available that you can use during announcement times at weekly services leading up to the Free Preview.

Brochures

You may also request a set of 50 preprinted color brochures and three preprinted color posters.

Testimonies

Allow those who have experienced the value of FPU for themselves to share their stories.

Additional Promotion Ideas:

- Newspaper Ads - Trade out free advertising for one FPU Membership Kit.
- Local Radio Stations may help promote FPU, especially those broadcasting *The Dave Ramsey Show*. Go to the Coordinator Resource Center at daveramsey.com/fpucoordinator and download our free radio spots.
- Local and Cable TV Stations are always looking for stories they can follow or cover that are changing their community. You can invite them to attend the program and follow a family's progress throughout the program.
- Public Service Announcements are usually FREE on church bulletin boards, online message forums, cable community access channels, community sections of the local newspaper, and regional radio station community bulletin spots.

For a successful FPU promotional campaign, follow the Suggested Promotional Schedule on the next page.

Suggested Promotional Schedule

SIX WEEKS TO PREVIEW MEETING:

Print promotional items from the Promotion CD-ROM at your local print shop or in-house.

FOUR WEEKS TO PREVIEW:

Place posters, banners, doorhangers, table tents, etc. in strategic, high-traffic areas around your church and community. Send postcards to church attendees. Place an ad in the local newspaper; advertise on your church website and newsletter.

THREE WEEKS TO PREVIEW:

Begin placing inserts in bulletins for church services. Also, show a one-minute video from the Promotional Videos DVD. You may want to have a high-influence church leader announce the upcoming Free Preview.

TWO WEEKS TO PREVIEW:

Continue with bulletin inserts. Show another promo video to your church. Have an email sent from the church to the congregation about the class.

ONE WEEK TO PREVIEW:

Have an FPU class graduate share a personal testimony or show another promo video to your church assembly. Have another high-influence church leader announce the upcoming Free Preview.

WEEK OF THE PREVIEW:

This is the optimal time for your minister to encourage the church to come to the Free Preview session. For maximum impact, the minister might consider teaching on becoming debt-free for the Kingdom! FPU will then be a natural follow-up to your minister's vision.

AS YOUR CLASS BEGINS:

Encourage your class members to invite friends and family to an open-house during Lesson #4. Doing so will cultivate future ministry and get folks excited about joining your church's next class!

Fill in YOUR Promotional Schedule on the next page!

SIX WEEKS TO PREVIEW MEETING

FOUR WEEKS TO PREVIEW MEETING

THREE WEEKS TO PREVIEW MEETING

TWO WEEKS TO PREVIEW MEETING

ONE WEEK TO PREVIEW MEETING

WEEK OF PREVIEW MEETING

CLASS START

The Free Preview

Prior to the Free Preview, please download and print a Class Enrollment Registration sheet from the Coordinator Resource Center at daveramsey.com/fpucoordinator.

Introduction Information (5 minutes)

- Welcome everyone and introduce yourself as the Class Coordinator.
- Be sure they understand that you are the host and facilitator of the program, NOT a financial instructor, advisor or counselor.
- Dave Ramsey will be the instructor via video DVD.
- Tell them why you have become a volunteer FPU Coordinator.

Start the Preview Video Presentation (25 minutes)

- Play the FPU Church Preview all the way through.
- Ask the following discussion questions:
  1. Why were the families in the video willing to make changes in their lives?
     Hopefully you'll hear, "They were serious about taking the steps necessary to getting out of debt, staying out of debt, and building wealth God's way!"
  2. How would it feel to manage your family's money and know you are making the right decisions?
     Hopefully you'll hear, "That would feel great!"
  3. Are you willing to invest what you might spend on pizza and colas for a month in order to change your family tree?
     You probably won't hear anything now. That one was rhetorical.

Invite Everyone to Enroll in This Life-Changing Program (10 minutes)

- The retail amount for the Membership Kits is $199.
- The church group discount is $93. (Shipping and handling is 7%. This amount can be added to the individual price or paid by the church.)
- Let them know that you will be ordering the class materials based upon the number of enrollments.

Announce the Time and Day Your First Class Will Start (5 minutes)

- See if anyone has questions.
- See Preview Frequently Asked Questions Reference Sheet (right).

Preview Frequently Asked Questions

How often do the classes meet?

There are 13 class sessions that meet one day per week.

How long is each class session?

- We suggest two hours for each weekly session.
- **Part One** presents the video teaching by Dave Ramsey to help you learn how to make wise financial decisions based on Scripture.
- **Part Two** of each class session is a small group discussion, with the class members sitting in a circle.
- The design of the small discussion groups helps you apply the principles to your daily life. The small group members will help hold each other accountable and support one another. The discussion group will help ensure we are working on the behavior part.

What is the average size of the class?

The video portion of the class is UNLIMITED. However, we recommend you break down into small groups of 8-12 families for the small group time with a coordinator/small group facilitator for each group.

What happens if a class member misses one class? Can they make it up?

If a class member misses a class session, he or she can make up the lesson by borrowing the DVD from the class coordinator. Also, every FPU membership kit contains an audio CD library of all 13 lessons for review.

What is included in the FPU Membership Kit?

See Page 8.

Can I get CEU (Continuing Education Unit) credit for the class?

Yes! In many cases, FPU can award CEU credit to class graduates. Go to daveramsey.com for details.

Preview Frequently Asked Questions

What if people have a previous version of the FPU materials?

People with previous versions of FPU are considered Lifetime Members and may attend your class at no additional charge. If they would like to upgrade their materials, call your advisor for details.

When will the first class start?

Please give them your start date. The FIRST CLASS SESSION usually takes place approximately TWO WEEKS after the final preview session, allowing time to process the enrollments and ship ALL the class materials.

Can your class member get additional assistance if they need it?

For more detailed, complex assistance, Dave Ramsey Certified Counselors offer discounts for one-on-one counseling. To find a counselor in your area, go to daveramsey.com/fpu/counseling.

Who benefits from this program?

Everyone truly benefits from this program regardless of your age or income, and whether you are single, married, divorced, or a single parent.

How much does this program cost?

Materials retail for $199. Church families pay $93 plus shipping and handling.

Who can attend with my Financial Peace membership?

Your spouse and teens living in the home.

Is there any refund if I do not like the program?

Our guarantee is simply this:

If you do it, **it works!** If you don't do it, **it won't work!**
If you will work the program, **you won't want your money back!**
If you don't work the program, **you don't get your money back!**